DEATHBULGE VOL.1
PRETTIER ON
THE OUTSIDE

BY DAN MARTIN

First paperback edition: September 2014
ISBN: 978-0-9930449-0-8

Designed and published by Dan Martin
Printed and bound by CPI Group (UK) Ltd, Croydon, CR0 4YY

CONTENTS

INTRODUCTION

For a while I had this vague belief that creating and maintaining a webcomic would be something I'd be good at if I really went for it, so eventually I gave myself a nice big slap in the face and got on with it. I began writing down ideas as they came to me and drew up a bunch. I showed them to a few friends and they were generally well-received. A promising start I thought. Maybe this will actually go somewhere. But what happened over the next couple years went way beyond my expectations, GOD DAMN.

So now here we are, A BOOK!! Deathbulge has finally made it into the print world. Oh this is very exciting indeed. Being the first of hopefully many, this is a super special book as the comics inside date back to the very beginning. A showcase of how Deathbulge has evolved from a string of sloppy comics, to a triumphant collection of not-so-sloppy comics.

Deathbulge has always been something I've taken very seriously and as the support from you all has grown, as has my determination to make every comic as good as it can be. Hopefully it shows! I'd hate to think I've let you guys down in any way. Only the best for my sexy readers.

I'd also like to take this opportunity to apologise to a handful of my friends, who have been subjected to my relentless displays of insecurity as I show them comic idea after comic idea and panic when they don't put enough "ha"s in their response. "Hahaha" or more is fine, anything less than "haha" is danger zone.

Again, thanks so much for buying my book and I hope it doesn't disappoint! If it does, feel free to let me know and I'll be sure to respond with a photo of me crying at your message.

— Dan

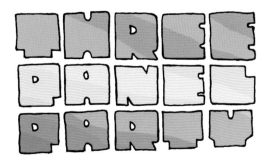

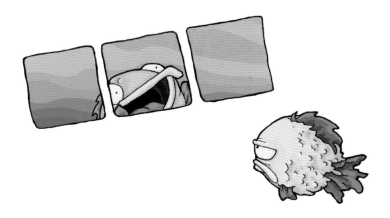

Now they'll never win that 9am staying awake contest.

Every now and then I like to go down to the toiletries section of the local supermarket and squirt out as much product from as many bottles as I can before I get arrested. It's not right letting them sit there like that for so long.

He should've died, but his body refused to conform to conventional symptoms of severe blood loss.

"Actually while you're here, does this look normal to you?"

Phil has a severe phobia of artificial light sources.

That psychologist is too good. A friend of mine went to see him the other month because of a phobia of cats. Now he eats them all the time.

Always say no to strangers.

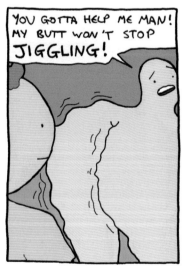

Within days the entire human population was jiggling.

What he didn't realise, was that it wasn't the illusion that won the ladies over. It was the custard. No lady can resist huddling up close to a hefty slather of that sugary yellow goodness. Custard is so tasty, so sexy. Man I'm getting excited just thinking about it.

"Ohh well, you can't please everyone." THAT'S LOSER TALK.

Wouldn't wanna dirty that fine thing on any Goomba heads no sir.

What's the point in waiting til the new year to do something when you can just as easily do it now? Not that I'm gonna do that either.

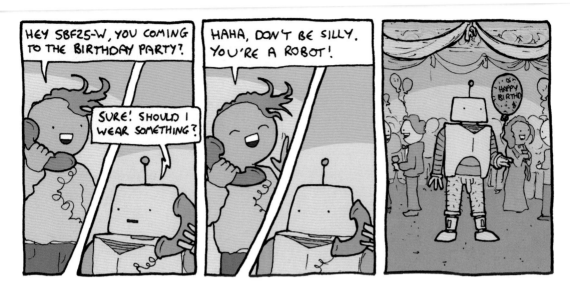

I'd like to take this opportunity to announce that for a reasonable fee, I will come to your birthday party dressed up like this and entertain guests with my unprecedented balloon holding skills.

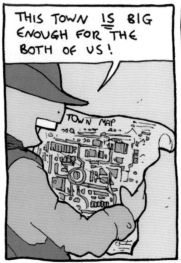

Still not sure how he won the stand-off with a town map.

BACK TO THE START

"I know it plays like crap but MAN does it sound great on my grass-shaped amplifier!"

Bren always makes sure to superglue his butt to the boat so that the fish don't pull him into the lake.

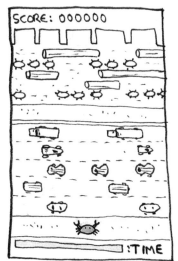

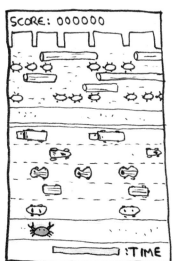

Great game. I had hours of fun walking slowly to the right in sync with the time gauge.

It's a great album. Chad Kroeger's yodelling halfway through Hakuna Matata is really something.

Ahh he'll be fine. Bowlers always get two goes.

Some suggest that he should just lean back. But how? This is Spiderman, not Leanman.

I hear the actress won an Oscar for that scene. Well deserved.

You think pitching a tent is embarrassing? Try pitching a gazebo.

For an extra £10, he'll take the blame for whatever godforsaken odours you produce.

Simmer rushed home and played that bass all through the night,
oblivious to the fact that he was keeping up the whales next door.

What was the bear doing behind the bush? TAKING ALL BETS! Odds list: Collecting twigs 5—
Ashamed of the ridiculous trousers his mother insisted he wear 30—1. Knocking one out 2—

Looks like the school BULLY needs to go to bully SCHOOL. Eh?? EH?!?!

Word has it that the chef fills the kitchen with smooth jazz whilst preparing this dish.

NEARBY, A GAMES COMPANY CAUSES AN UPROAR WITH ITS LATEST FIGHTING GAME.

PUNCH SLAP GAMES

PERVS! THE LOT O' YER!

TWATS!

WOMEN ARE MORE THAN JUST A PAIR OF NICE TITS

I'M QUITE PARTIAL TO RUBBER BALLS BUT THE BOOBS IN THE GAME ARE JUST TOO... BOUNCY!

SIR! THESE PROTESTS ARE GETTING OUT OF HAND! WE NEED TO TONE DOWN THE OVER-SEXUALIZATION OF THE FEMALE CHARACTERS.

FIGHTING FIGHTERS

THAT IS NOT AN OPTION. OVER-SEXUALIZATION IS WHAT'S SELLING THESE GAMES!

I didn't need a reference photo for that last panel,
all I had to do was look down and draw what I saw.

The cool thing about that site is, if you're feeling REALLY filthy.
There's another page you can go on where 'porn' is written in red font.

I get quite a lot of messages from people telling me they didn't understand this one. If you look at it long enough I'm sure you'll get it eventually. BUT, if you've already been staring at it for an hour and you're beginning to lose your sanity. Check the bottom of page 240 for a massive hint.

Consider yourself lucky he didn't share it.

"Down low?? TOO SLO-*wakes up in a hand-shaped crater*

When I was younger, I used to go through a phase where I'd flush the toilet while talking to people on the phone, even though I hadn't actually been using the toilet. Gold.

I was gonna make more ball jokes, but I never got ROUND to it.   ...I'll see myself out.

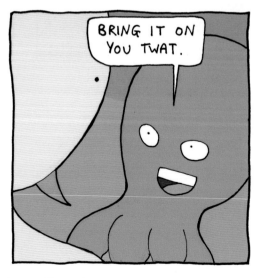

"Sorry but I'd like to return this pen please. The judgemental eyes he gave me as I wrote down unhealthy items on my shopping list were just too much to bear."

It doesn't have to stop there. Consider de-shelling enough pistachios to fill a swimming pool and then swan dive into that shit.

DECEMBER JUST WOULDN'T BE DECEMBER WITHOUT MY DAILY ADVENT CALENDAR CHOCOLATE!

HAH! YOU CALL **THAT** AN ADVENT CALENDAR?!!

COME WITH ME IF YOU WANNA SEE A **REAL** ADVENT CALENDAR.

KNOCK! KNOCK!

EXCUSE ME MISS, BUT I BELIEVE IT'S THE 7th TODAY?

It's a shame that they only go up to 24; effectively making Christmas Day feel like the biggest let down ever. No present is gonna top 24 days of lay, unless it's a copy of Sega Bass Fishing of course.

OH WOW! DEATHBULGE IS WINNING THE POLL FOR **COOLEST BAND!**

DEATHBULGE:
HERE'S WALLY!:
FUNK DUNGUS:
SHIT BAND:
BACKRUP GRANDAD:
FISTFUL OF FISTS:

I WOULDN'T GET TOO EXCITED, THE HIPSTER VOTES HAVEN'T BEEN COUNTED YET.

THERE YOU GO!

GOD DAMMIT...

DEATHBULGE:
HERE'S WALLY!:
FUNK DUNGUS:
SHIT BAND:
BACKRUP GRANDAD:
FISTFUL OF FISTS:

I never shared this comic before because I felt that hipster jokes were getting stale. But hopefully by the time this book is out, hipster jokes will be so dated that this strip will have some sort of vintage charm to it.

The headphones allow him to really feel the bass of those booming job opportunities.

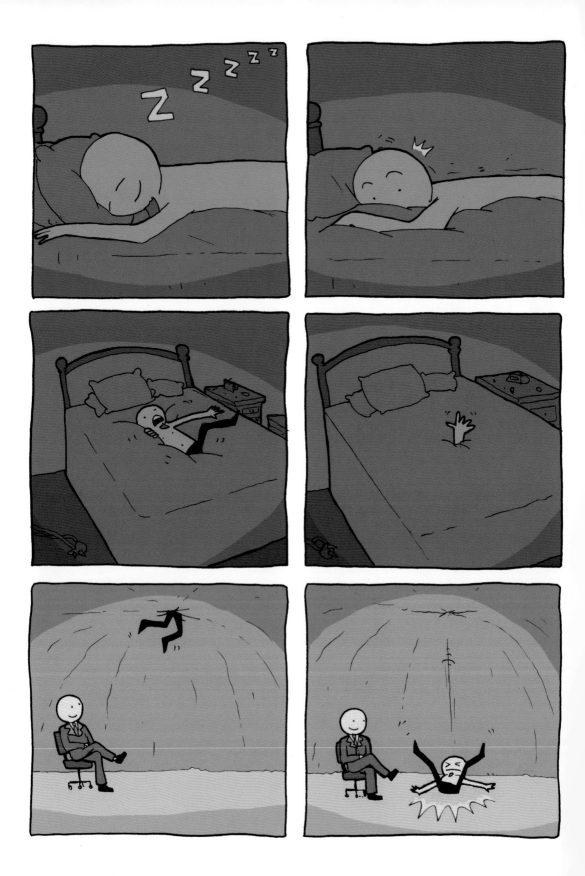

"I'm glad you're here though. Now that there's two of us, I can finally work on my alley-oops."

AHH.. NOTHING LIKE A QUIET NIGHT IN ON HALLOWEEN.

DING DONG!

TRICK OR TREAT!!!

LITTLE SHITS

WELL, I DON'T HAVE ANY **TREATS**, SO A **TRICK** IT'LL HAVE TO BE!

THAT'S FINE TOO.

OKAY, PICK A CARD, BUT **DON'T SHOW ME!**

FANTASTIC, NOW PUT IT BACK IN THE DECK FACE DOWN.

It's a shame he didn't pick a face card. Would've made for a far more interesting corpse.

"Noo guys, come back! You didn't finish the urethra!
HOW THE HELL AM I SUPPOSED TO PEE??"

Gravity (9.8m/s²) x Time (in seconds) = Wet face.

Hopefully he'll find some nice low-fat fish closer to the seabed.

WHOAAA HEY BABY, WASSAPPENIN'?

WHAT SAY WE DITCH YOUR HORSE-FACED FRIEND AND SET YOU UP WITH A NICE PAIR OF MY BALLS IN YOUR MOUTH?

UGH!! WHY ARE YOU SUCH A **JERK?!!**

IF IT WASN'T FOR PEOPLE LIKE ME, YOU WOULDN'T APPRECIATE PEOPLE WHO **WEREN'T** JERKS, AS THERE'D BE NO JERKS TO COMPARE THEM TO. I'M MERELY DOING MY PART FOR SOCIETY.

TAKE ME NOW YOU SAINT!

If someone answers your question in the same way that this guy did. Sleep with them immediately. They're clearly a fan of Deathbulge, and Deathbulge fans deserve the best.

49

His iPod is stored in the same place that Sonic stores his rings.

Now that he's orbiting Earth. I guess he really is SEEING THEM AROUND.

...and yet it still made it into the book somehow.

MAN... WHAT IF I PUNCHED HER IN THE FACE RIGHT NOW? IN FRONT OF ALL OUR FRIENDS...

IT WOULD OBVIOUSLY CREATE A VERY UNPLEASANT AND AWKWARD SCENARIO. BUT THE IDEA OF DOING SOMETHING THAT WOULD HAVE SUCH AN IMMEDIATE IMPACT ON THE ATMOSPHERE FASCINATES ME.

WE'RE HAVING A PLEASANT DISCUSSION, SHE'S A LOVELY PERSON, I HAVE ABSOLUTELY **NO** REASON TO HIT HER, BUT THAT JUST MAKES THE IDEA OF DOING IT ALL THE MORE INTRIGUINGLY BIZARRE.

AH, WHO AM I KIDDING? I THINK LIKE THIS EVERY NOW AND THEN, BUT I NEVER DO IT. I WONDER IF THERE'LL EVER BE A DAY WHERE I ACTUALLY DO IT.

MAYBE TODAY IS THE DAY, OH GOD THIS COULD BE IT! RIGHT HERE! DOO IT! **I'M GOING FOR IT!!**

WHAP

OH GOD I ACTUALLY DID IT! THIS IS **INSANE!** THEY'RE REALLY ANGRY.... OF COURSE THEY WOULD BE...

OH MAN THIS IS SO WEIRD. WHAT IF I JUST KEPT THIS GOING?

WHAT IF I JUST LIKE, GOT NAKED RIGHT NOW, AND AND STOOD STILL, WITHOUT SAYING A WORD... HAHAH, THEY WOULD SO NOT KNOW WHAT TO DO.

MIGHT AS WELL, I'M IN THE ZONE NOW.

I'm waiting for the day that I'm greeted by a fan who just flat out punches me in the face whilst shouting "WHAP!". They'll burst into laughter and ask me if I understood the reference. I'll confirm that I did and attempt to laugh it off as I pass out in a pool of blood.

It's okay, a few graphic stories about dry surfaces will clean this mess up.

You'd be pretty sad too if all your friends were cut up in front of you and there was nothing you could do about it.

Due to no longer existing, he no longer goes back in time to put off his parents from having a kid, so they have a kid, and the cycle continues indefinitely. THIS COMIC MAKES PERFECT SENSE.

He's not very good at turning corners.

... AND THAT'S WHY I ALWAYS PUT THE EGGS IN **FIRST**!

HAHA, FAIR ENOUGH!

OH GOD!! WHAT'S HAPPENING RIGHT NOW?!!

A GAP IN CONVERSATION?

YEAH BUT... WHY IS IT SO UNBEARABLY **QUIET**?!?!

MAYBE BECAUSE THERE'S NO EAR-SHATTERING CLUB MUSIC TO MASK THE AWKWARD SILENCES.

I GUESS... BUT HOW COME WE RAN OUT OF THINGS TO TALK ABOUT SO SOON?!

PROBABLY BECAUSE WE HAVEN'T SPENT HALF THE TIME SHOUTING "WHAT?!" AND REPEATING OURSELVES.

GOOD **HEAVENS**, YOU'RE RIGHT!! **THIS SUCKS!!**

"I'm so glad we moved to this horribly hot and stuffy club. I have trouble talking to girls if I'm not sweating profusely at the same time."

We're gonna need a bigger washing machine.

"Damn girl, you put the ASS in Jurassic.

"Maybe I should just link you to the site that the joke is on.
Here: http://www.hahaHAHAHFUCK.com"

THE ADVENTURES OF **THE GUY THAT CAN'T GET ANYTHING RIGHT.**

YO BRUNSWICK, DID YOU REMEMBER TO BRING THE TOOL BOX??

YES

SWEET MAN! NICE ONE!

DAMN. I WAS SUPPOSED TO FORGET IT.

Hi everyone! Brunswick here. To celebrate my Deathbulge de
To celebrate my Deathbulge d
I've been put in charge of
this comic's accompanying
text
I hope

WHEYY!! MY GAME CAME!

AND SO DID I

SEGA BASS FISHING

WAIT WHAT?!! NO INSTRUCTION MANUAL?!! **NOW** WHAT AM I SUPPOSED TO READ WHILE ON THE TOILET?!!

WHAT ABOUT THE BACK COVER?

SEGA BASS FISH

SEGA BASS

It's a shame that game manuals are getting thinner and thinner these days. Making for some
rather underwhelming reading experiences. But hey, WORRY NOT, because now you have thi
sweet book of comics to see you through many a toilet visit

I'm surprised they managed to book a plane that lands there.

this up.

Don't you just hate it when this happens? I'm down to my third face already.

THIS IS A SWEET BOOK MAN! I'D BE HAPPY TO PUBLISH IT!

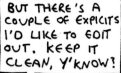

BUT THERE'S A COUPLE OF EXPLICITS I'D LIKE TO EDIT OUT. KEEP IT CLEAN, Y'KNOW?

LIKE WHAT?

FOR EXAMPLE, IN THE SENTENCE: "WE LEFT HIS BIKE ON THE ROOF FOR SHITS AND GIGGLES"...

DO WE **REALLY** NEED THE PHRASE "SHITS AND GIGGLES"?

WELL.. I GUESS NOT... BUT WHAT ALTERNATIVES ARE THERE??

HOW ABOUT DUMPS & CHUCKLES?!

W-WHAT?! NO!! OF COURSE NOT!

LOGS AND LAUGHTER?

NO!

MANURE AND MERRIMENT?

NO!!

OH! OH! HOW ABOUT COWPIES AND CACHINNATION?

I'M OUTTA HERE.

"Turds and tittering?? BUTTSNAKES AND BELLY LAUGHS?!?!"

YOU'VE TERRORIZED THIS CITY FOR LONG ENOUGH **TWO-FACE!**

UGH! I WISH PEOPLE WOULD STOP CALLING ME THAT!

I HAVE **TWO HALVES** OF A FACE. MATHEMATICALLY I SHOULD BE CALLED **ONE-FACE!**

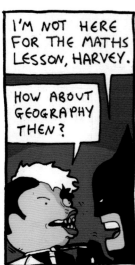

I'M NOT HERE FOR THE MATHS LESSON, HARVEY.

HOW ABOUT GEOGRAPHY THEN?

HMM... NOW THAT YOU MENTION IT. I HAVE BEEN MEANING TO BRUSH UP ON MY CAPITAL CITIES!

A WHILE LATER...

... SO, TO REVIEW! **GEORGETOWN** IS THE CAPITAL OF **GUYANA!** A HANDY WAY TO REMEMBER THIS IS THAT **GEORGE** IS A **GUY'S** NAME!

THAT **IS** HANDY!

Other handy ways to remember capital cities:
'Jordan is Amman's name' and 'Victoria sells Seychelles on the sea shore'.

No one was allowed to clean the vomit off their face until they were dared to

At least it's less disappointing than the future.

After about 20 minutes, José dressed up as an asteroid and slayed them both

They say that chewing ice is another sign of sexual frustration. Bollocks to that. When I go to a bar and get given a cocktail that's 50% blocks of ice. You can bet I'm gonna eat that shit too. You can call it sexual frustration if you want, I call it getting my money's worth.

In hindsight, maybe the airbags shouldn't have been made out of fishtanks either.

He never should have thrown so many shapes on the dance floor. That's how they get lost.

What follows is a special comic for which I asked readers to suggest lines of dialogue. I worked in as many as I could into a (hopefully) coherent story.

The reader-suggested lines are displayed in red text.

THEY ENTERED THE ROOM WITH CONFIDENCE, READY FOR ANYTHING.

THEY THOUGHT THEY HAD IT ALL FIGURED OUT...

BUT LITTLE DID THEY KNOW...

THAT IT WAS THE PARSNIP ALL ALONG!

WHOA!!

WHAT A TWIST!!

I LOVE THIS SHOW!

MY KEYS! I CAN'T FIND MY KEYS!!

WHAT DO THEY LOOK LIKE?

YOU KNOW, THE BLUE ONES!

HOLY SEA-MAMMALS!

THAT WAS A BIG NARWHAL!!

DID YOU SEE IT?! HUH?! SIMMER?? DID YOU?!!

NO I BLOODY WELL DIDN'T!

I AM DRIVING YOU KNOW. I GOTTA CONCENTRATE ON THE ROAD!

ESPECIALLY WHEN THERE'S A DINOSAUR RUNNING TOWARDS US.

SMASH!

CHOCOLATE

EURGH!! WHAT THE—? GOD DAMN THAT IS STICKY!

UGH, I HATE IT WHEN A DINOSAUR RAMS MY CAR AND IT'S TURNED INTO CHOCOLATE.

YEAH SAME.

GUYS! LOOK!! OVER THERE! IT'S THE SCHOOL!

AAHH!! HELP US!! HELLPP!!!

K.A.F.U.

WOW! DID YOU HEAR HER? SHE SOUNDED SO HOT!

PROBABLY BECAUSE SHE'S BURNING TO DEATH.

HAHA OH YEAH, RIGHT! GUESS WE'D BETTER GET TO WORK THEN, HUH!

AND SO...

BAM!

COME ON, WE'RE GETTING YOU LOT OUTTA HERE!

KAWAII AS FU...

THIS WAY!!

K.A.F.U.

WHEYYY!!

WE DID IT!! WE'RE TOTALLY HEROES!

YEAH!!

THANK GOD THE ANIMÉ SCHOOL GIRLS MADE IT OUT ALIVE.

WHO THE HELL ARE YOU?

I AM THE LIQUOR GENIE OF KARMIC JUSTICE, HERE TO REWARD YOUR BOUT OF HEROISM!

I UHH... I LOST MY PENIS TO WILD POLAR BEARS IN AUSTRALIA... YEAH..

EW! GROSS!! FORGET YOU THEN!

MAN SHE'S SEXY.

LENNOX! C'MON WE GOTTA GO GET BREN!

WHY, WHERE'D HE GO?

HE STORMED OFF TO THE MAYOR'S OFFICE TO DEMAND A REWARD.

A REWARD FOR ALL OF US??

NO, JUST HIM.

WHAT?! SELFISH BUGGER! LET'S GET GOING THEN!

....

MEANWHILE, AT THE MAYOR'S OFFICE.

86

WHY WOULD YOU JUST LEAVE YOUR TROUSERS HERE LIKE THIS?!!
IS THIS YOUR IDEA OF A **JOKE**?!

THE LLAMA THING I CAN DEAL WITH, BUT THIS IS GOING TOO FAR!

THERE MUST BE SOMETHING INCREDIBLY WRONG WITH YOUR BRAIN...

YOU HONESTLY DON'T UNDERSTAND IT, DO YOU?! I'M NOT JUST DOING THIS FOR THE HECK OF IT...

I'M PART OF A WHOLE COMMUNITY THAT DOES THIS, AND BELIEVE IT OR NOT, WE HAVE FUN DOING IT.

IT'S PART OF OUR NEW "TROUSERS SAY HELLO" ART MOVEMENT.

I'VE HEARD ENOUGH, I SAY WE BURN THEM AT THE STAKE.

THE TROUSERS?

YEAH.

AND SO...
STOP!! YOU'RE MAKING A BIG MISTAKE!!

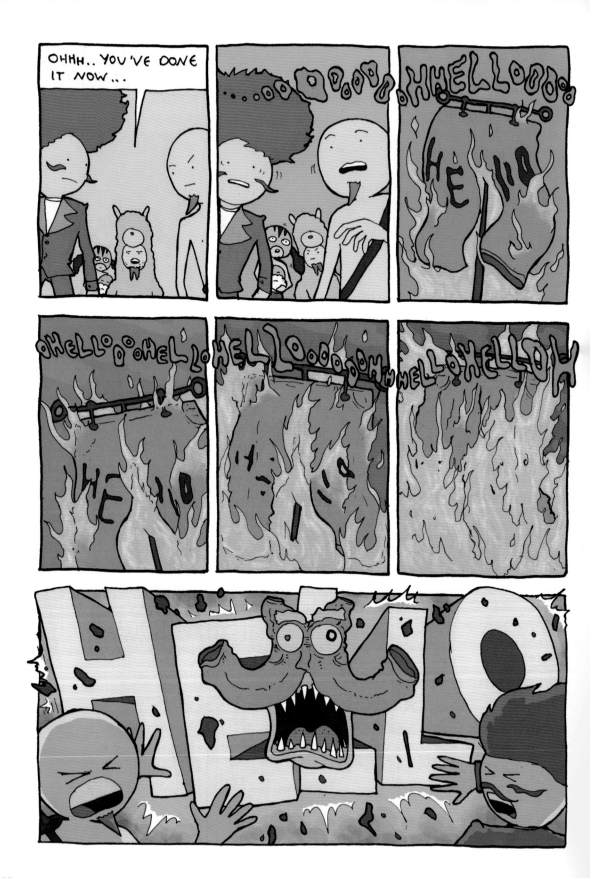

WELL, GUESS THERE'S NOTHING TO DO NOW BUT WAIT FOR DEATH!

YOU MIND EXPLAINING WHAT THE **HELL** IS GOING ON?!!

BASICALLY, YOU'VE DOOMED THE PLANET. WAY TO GO SON, PROUD OF YOU.

HA HA! EXACTLY!! AND THIS ISN'T EVEN MY FINAL FORM!!

WHAT **IS** YOUR FINAL FORM THEN?

WELL UH... GEE.. I... I DUNNO! I'VE NEVER HAD TO RESORT TO IT BEFORE!

THIS FORM IS USUALLY SUFFICIENT ENOUGH TO GET THINGS DONE.

UNFORTUNATELY I DON'T REALLY HAVE ANYTHING TO GIVE AS A REWARD...

HEY GUYS! LOOK! I FOUND PANDORA'S BOX IN THE CUPBOARD!

JUST CAUSE IT HAS QUESTION MARKS ON IT, DOESN'T MEAN IT'S PANDORA'S BOX.

OHH! I FORGOT ABOUT THAT! THAT WAS MEANT AS A PRESENT FOR SOMEONE AGES AGO!

HEY... HOW ABOUT YOU GUYS HAVE THAT AS YOUR REWARD?

DEAL!

OH BOY! I WONDER WHAT IT COULD BE!

I- IS THAT..?!

COULD IT BE ???

If Future Dan attempts to do this again for the 200th comic. Tell him he's an idiot.

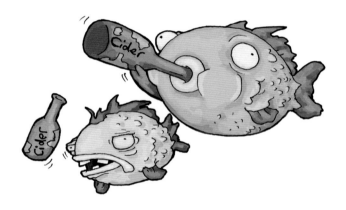

One thing I love about Dwayne's World Class Cider is the variety.
You'll never experience the same taste twice.

I DON'T KNOW WHY WE DON'T GO TO MORE MUSIC FESTIVALS... THEY'RE SUCH A GREAT EXPERIENCE.

EVERYONE'S GENERALLY MORE SOCIABLE, AND YOU CAN MEET SOME REALLY INTERESTING PEOPLE!

AS A RESULT, THE CAMPING FIELDS ALWAYS SEEM TO HAVE THIS UNIQUE MAGICAL AURA ABOUT THEM.

SOMETIMES IT'S WORTH JUST SITTING BACK AND SPEND SOME TIME SOAKING IN THE ATMOSPHERE.

OH AND YEAH THE MUSIC'S GOOD TOO I GUESS.

HEY BRO...

One time at a festival I woke up to the sound of a guy peeing on my tent. So I hit the part of the tent he was peeing on from the inside, resulting in it splashing back all over him. He was not happy, but I sure was. I wonder if he's reading this. HEY DUDE!

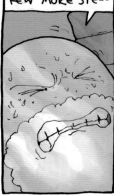

You haven't lived until you've had a whiff of festival bins on a hot day.

GUYS! **GUYS!!** I GOT YOU A PERFORMANCE SLOT ON THE "NEW TALENT" STAGE!

HOLY SHIT! HOW DID YOU MANAGE THAT?!

A BAND PULLED OUT, C'MON WE GOTTA HURRY!!

BUT WE DIDN'T BRING ANY EQUIPMENT!

DON'T WORRY ABOUT THAT. THEY HAVE EVERYTHING YOU'LL NEED BACKSTAGE.

MOMENTS LATER...

WOW.. SO THIS IS IT... OUR TIME TO SHINE HAS FINALLY COME...

WOO!

YEAHH!!

EARDRUM-PIERCING WHISTLES

ALRIGHT Y'ALL! WE'RE GONNA KICK THINGS OFF WITH A SINGLE OFF OUR NEW ALBUM!

WAIT A MINUTE... WE DON'T **HAVE** A NEW ALBUM...

WE DON'T HAVE **ANY** ALBUMS!!

Was this incident the kick up the arse that Deathbulge needed? Does this mean they'll finally start writing music and developing their career?? Don't get your hopes up.

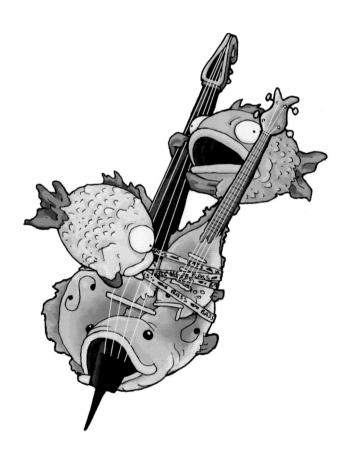

"...and that's not all! GAZE IN WONDER AS I RUN MY FINGER THROUGH THE FLAME WITHOUT BURNING MYSELF!"

"This tastes familiar..."

If you're curious how to pronounce the name of that tomato shop, it goes like this:
To-may-toe, to-mah-toe, too-mah-tur, toe-meh-chuh.

For best results, include two burgers in the process and pretend that the second burger is a partner watching in horror as their loved one is eaten alive.

Of course he's gay. If he wasn't, Virgin Mary wouldn't be called Virgin Mary.

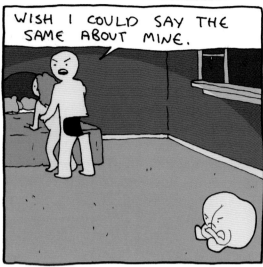

Not a day goes by where I don't thank mine for sticking by me.

"I want people to know how great I am at doing selfless things for selfish reasons."

"Wow dude your punches are AWFUL!"

WELL, **FALUS**.. WHAT CAN I SAY?? I'M IMPRESSED! GREAT HAIR... PASSION FOR ADVENTURE... AN OUTFIT THAT WILL BE A PAIN IN THE ARSE FOR COSPLAYERS TO REPLICATE...

RPG
MAIN ★ CHARACTER AUDITIONS
★ * TODAY!! ★

YOU HAVE ALL THE MAKINGS OF A **SUPERB** PROTAGONIST!!

BUT WHAT ABOUT YOUR PARENTS, HOW ARE <u>THEY</u> DOING?

BOTH OF THEM ARE ALIVE AND WELL!

GET OUT OF MY SIGHT.

"Kill them and we'll talk."

WOW! LOOK AT ALL THIS COOL CRAP! WHAT A GREAT STORE!

WHOA!! A DECK OF PLAYING CARDS!!

I'VE ALWAYS WANTED TO PLAY SOLITAIRE WITH REAL CARDS!

I'LL TAKE THESE, PLEASE!

VERY WELL..

BUT BE WARNED, FOR THIS IS A CURSED DECK!

IT IS?!

WELL SORT OF, FOR THE MOST PART THEY'RE NO DIFFERENT FROM A NORMAL DECK OF CARDS.

BUT WHATEVER YOU DO... DON'T PLAY SOLITAIRE.

GO TO HELL!! I'M TAKING THESE HOME TO PLAY SOLITAIRE!

FUCK SAKE.

It's a shame the cards don't do that anymore when you win. Newer computers just give you some lame-ass fireworks. How could you do that to us Solitaire?? THAT WAS THE BEST PART. THAT WAS YOUR IDENTITY.

He was crowned king the moment he left the parlour.

I FEARED THIS DAY WOULD COME...

I'VE BEEN SO ADDICTED TO THE FEELING OF NOSTALGIA... I'VE RUN OUT OF THINGS TO FEEL NOSTALGIC ABOUT!!

I'VE INDULGED IN ABSOLUTELY **EVERYTHING** FROM MY CHILDHOOD!

DOES THAT MEAN I HAVE NO CHOICE BUT TO MOVE ON WITH MY LIFE AND FOCUS ON THE FUTURE??

OH MAN, I REMEMBER THE **FIRST TIME** I NOSTALGIA'D OVER THIS! **THOSE WERE THE DAYS.**

"Oh dude, do you remember when we were all sat in the pub reminiscing about that time we reminisced about when we all got kicked out of a pub for reminiscing too loudly? GOOD TIMES."

"HE DIVED REF I SWEAR."

"How long have you been standing there like that?"
"NOT LONG ENOUGH."

He's lucky the hook went through the side of his mouth.
Ahh man, imagine it going through your gums, UGHUGHGHUGH.

"Alright alright, I'll drop it down to £9. but only because of those sweet candle tricks you showed me the other day."

118

After a few pubs they went to a late night cinema screening
and sat in the front row. Everyone complained.

... SO ANYWAY, TO CUT A LONG STORY SHORT. NOW ALL THREE OF THEM ARE PREGNANT.

WHOA DUDE!! YOU SERIOUS?!! MY JAW HAS **LITERALLY** HIT THE FLOOR!

UGH, NO IT HASN'T. I HATE IT WHEN PEOPLE DON'T USE THAT WORD PROPERLY.

HEH, THIS WOULD BE A RATHER HUMOUROUS COMIC IF MY JAW WAS ACTUALLY TOUCHING THE FLOOR...

HA HA

BUT IT'S NOT.

THOOM!

GOOD LORD!

THE PUNCHLINE ENFORCER!!

SORRY I'M LATE.

NOW LET'S GET THAT JAW ON THE FLOOR.

Nice to see the Punchline Enforcer finally invading my comics.
Could've used his help on some of my earlier comics though, yeesh.

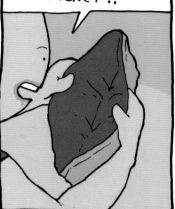

BUT THERE'S ST--!!!

COULD IT...
COULD IT BE?!
...I FINISHED THE TORTILLA CHIPS AND THE DIP AT THE SAME TIME?!!

WOW WHAT A BEAUTIFUL MOMENT.

THIS CALLS FOR A CELEBRATION!!

If you're wondering what he's listening to in the last panel. It's just a simple bass groove overlaid with recordings of people eating huge burgers as loudly as possible.

"Oh and he totally saw what you were doing when I left the house earlier. Don't do that.

What a stupid theory. Everyone knows the real way to tell if someone
is good in bed is if they're wearing an official Deathbulge t-shirt.

"Okay Rob, your turn. I dare you to phone an ambulance.

He just couldn't resist that voluptuous dorsel fin.

HUH, THAT'S PRETTY INTERESTING ACTUALLY!

POUR

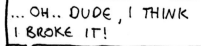

...OH.. DUDE, I THINK I BROKE IT!

IT POURED COLD WATER, AND THAT'S EXACTLY WHAT I WAS EXPECTING IT TO DO!

THAT'S BECAUSE YOU WERE EXPECTING IT TO KEEP DOING THE UNEXPECTED.

...AND WHAT'S THE OPPOSITE OF DOING THE UNEXPECTED??

I'd love to elaborate on what the kettle would've done next had Lennox not binned it so soon. But frankly I have no idea where to go after that last bit. I mean I guess he'd lose track eventually of what to expect the kettle to pour temperature-wise, but he'd know that it would pour water, that much is certain. So maybe that would be when it starts pouring the OPPOSITE of water. But what even IS the opposite of water? Something really dry I guess? SANDPAPER?? Though you can't really pour that can you? Haha man I dunno. Let's just go to the next comic shall we? Yeah.

He then went off to prank girls into kissing frogs.
Not the poisonous ones of course, that just wouldn't be cool.

Apparently it's good luck to read Deathbulge comics every day whilst touching your tongue with your knee.

"Sorry Bren, I think that's bigger than 100ml, you're gonna have to leave that behind."

This device is currently in flames. Close any programs or explosions that might be burning the device, and then try again.

GREETINGS ONE AND ALL!

I AM BUFFASUS! THE BEING OF UNLIMITED KNOWLEDGE AND WISDOM!

PRESENT TO ME YOUR UNANSWERABLE QUESTIONS, AND I SHALL ANSWER THEM...

YES, YOU THERE WITH THE JUMPER!

HI YEAH, SO LIKE, Y'KNOW WHEN SOMEONE MAKES A STATUS ON FACEBOOK ABOUT SOMETHING UNFORTUNATE LIKE THEIR PET DYING OR WHATEVER...

... DO I LIKE THE STATUS? CAUSE IT SEEMS LIKE A DECENT WAY TO GIVE CONSOLATION...

BUT I WORRY THAT THEY'LL THINK THAT I LIKE THEIR SADNESS...

GULP!

... M-MAYBE I SHOULD JUST LEAVE A COMMENT...

Buffasus comes from a parallel universe where I actually bother to shade people in.

ALL YOU CAN EAT?! NOW WE'RE TALKING!

HAHA,

HMHMM.

HEH.

WHOA WHOA **WHOA!** STOP EVERYTHING! WHAT THE HELL WAS THAT?!

YOU CALL THAT "STUDIO LAUGHTER"?? VIEWERS WON'T FEEL COMFORTABLE LAUGHING ALONG WITH **THAT** NOW WILL THEY?!

WELL COME ON, YOU CAN'T SERIOUSLY EXPECT US TO ROAR WITH LAUGHTER AT MOST OF THESE JOKES..

I MEAN, IT'S NOT EXACTLY AMBITIOUS HUMOUR IS IT? YOU'RE JUST MAKING BASIC JOKES BASED ON EACH CHARACTER'S GIMMICK.

YEAH EXACTLY.

LIKE WITH THE BIG GUY, EVERY JOKE HE MAKES IS ABOUT EATING LOTS AND BEING FAT.

HAHA YEAH, IT'S VERY ONE-DIMENSIONAL.

HELL I PROBABLY COULD'VE WRITTEN THIS MYSELF.

BLAM

134

They had previously tried to use canned laughter.
But that kept questioning the quality of the jokes too.

"Actually while I have the book out, I'm gonna see if 'bin' is a word too. Pretty sure you cheated somewhere."

SOMETIMES PEOPLE ASK ME "HOW DO YOU MAKE YOUR COMICS?"

WELL THERE'S TWO PARTS TO THIS PROCESS. GETTING THE IDEAS, AND MAKING THEM INTO COMICS..

THE FIRST PART IS ALL DOWN TO MY PAL IAN THE FISHERMAN.

HEY THERE!

IAN GOES OUT TO A MYSTERIOUS LAKE EVERY WEEK...

WHERE FISH HAVE JOKES INSCRIBED ON THEIR BODIES.

THE FISH CAN BE VERY SELECTIVE ABOUT WHAT THEY'LL BITE. FOR EXAMPLE A FISH WITH A PUN ON IT'S BODY, WOULD ONLY GO FOR WORDPLAY LURES.

EW GROSS.

OBSERVATION

LIMP BRISKET

BUT LUCKILY IAN IS KITTED OUT WITH ALL KINDS OF LURES.

HE'S PREPARED FOR ANYTHING.

HE'S PREPARED FOR ANYTHING.

IAN TENDS TO STAY OUT AT THE LAKE FOR A LONG TIME TO CATCH AS MANY FISH AS POSSIBLE.

BECAUSE EVEN THOUGH HE ONLY NEEDS TO BRING BACK TWO FISH A WEEK FOR THE MONDAY AND FRIDAY UPDATES..

...IF HE CATCHES MORE, HE CAN AFFORD TO BE PICKY ABOUT WHICH JOKES TO BRING BACK...

AND IN DOING SO, KEEP UP A GOOD STANDARD.

ONCE HE RETURNS, I CONGRATULATE HIM ON A JOB WELL DONE..

...AND GIVE HIM A HANDFUL OF COOL STICKERS AS THANKS.

(I USED TO GIVE HIM MONEY, BUT HE SEEMS TO LIKE THE STICKERS A LOT MORE.)

I THEN STUFF THE FISH WITH VARIOUS PENS AND COLOURED INKS..

AND EAT IT RAW.

THE NEXT STEP IS TO THROW UP ON A LARGE CANVAS. THIS IS WHERE IT GETS A LITTLE ICKY.

LUCKILY THE MIX OF RAW FISH AND INKS ARE HORRIBLE ENOUGH TO MAKE ME BARF AUTOMATICALLY.

WHICH SAVES ME FROM HAVING TO RAM MY FINGERS DOWN MY THROAT.

I LOVE BEING ABLE TO CUT CORNERS LIKE THAT.

I THEN TAKE A PHOTO OF THE RESULTING MESS.

...AND TRANSFER IT TO THE COMPUTER!

(I USED TO USE A SCANNER, BUT IT DOESN'T WORK ANYMORE).

ANYWAY, NOW THAT THE IMAGE IS ON THE COMPUTER. I BEGIN POLISHING IT UP IN PHOTOSHOP.

AFTER A FEW TWEAKS, THE COMIC IS READY TO BE POSTED ON THE SITE!

AND THERE YOU HAVE IT!

I'm selling the original canvases if anyone is interested.

I'd rather save my batteries for more important things. Like my electric pencil sharpener that's shaped like a giant pencil. So cool

You should always shake people's hands, even if you're super sweaty. It's an important symbol of friendliness and trust. You may worry that the recipient will judge you for having sweaty hands and pull a disgusted face, but that is far from reality. When they shake your hand, they will realise how sweaty you are. They will realise how hard you must have fought to overcome your insecurity about your sweatiness in order to shake their hand. They will appreciate your bravery. They will embrace the sweat. They will thank you for the sweat. They will cry tears of happiness and for years to come they will tell all their friends about you and that defining moment in which you displayed such sweaty valiance.

The females also have secret udder compartments that they rent out for drug stashing.

The key is to sleep in an airtight box. I mean sure, you'll suffocate in your sleep, but no spiders will get to you!

Suddenly, Ricardo's enthusiasm for Pete's mystery burgers dropped considerably.

If you wish to add jelly or jam. Simply shove it up your nose and be ready to sneeze as the toast transfers to your mouth.

146

"Nuts to this, I'm off to explore that tomb for 38 seconds."

147

The key is to end everything with "lol jk jk 😊 YOU KNOW I LOVE YOU REALLY 😊😊

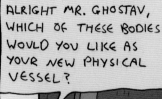

ALRIGHT MR. GHOSTAV, WHICH OF THESE BODIES WOULD YOU LIKE AS YOUR NEW PHYSICAL VESSEL?

THERE'S THE INCREDIBLY HANDSOME AND BUFF **OPTION A...**

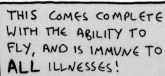

THIS COMES COMPLETE WITH THE ABILITY TO FLY, AND IS IMMUNE TO **ALL** ILLNESSES!

.. AND THEN THERE'S OPTION B THAT HAS A BIG DICK.

OPTION B! OPTION B!!

THOUGH THIS ONE IS IN VERY BAD SHAPE AND IS LIABLE TO FREQUENT HEART ATTACKS.

BIG DICK.

IN FACT I'M NOT EVEN SURE WHY WE'RE OFFERING THIS OPTION.

IS DEBIT CARD OKAY?

Option A isn't that great anyway; doesn't even have chest hair.

"Well that didn't work. But at least now I can lick my elbow."

Limit Break Level 4: Omnisexual.

For the most extreme cases of bull passivity. There's a special cape that has a very interesting article printed on it. How does this enrage the bull you ask? Well come on, if you were trying to read something but couldn't because it kept being flapped about by some jerk, you'd wanna headbutt someone too.

I'll never understand why people actually do that. Then again, there's a lot of silly things people do that I can't comprehend but HEY LET'S NOT GET INTO THAT HERE.

Dedicated to one of my mum's elephant figurines that I accidentall
smashed as a kid. To this day the feelings of guilt remain. **RLF**

AT LAST.. AFTER **YEARS** OF SEARCHING... I'VE FINALLY FOUND YOU...

IS IT TRUE WHAT THEY SAY? THAT YOU HAVE IN YOUR POSSESSION THE "**ULTIMATE CHRISTMAS JUMPER**"??

IT SURE IS!

IN THAT CASE, I WOULD LIKE TO BUY IT.

COOL! I'LL GO GET IT FOR YOU.

MERRY CHRISTMAS

On the back side of the jumper there's an advent calendar where every door has a tiny christmas jumper inside.

AND JUST WHAT DO YOU THINK YOU'RE DOING??

HO HO HOOOO! I'M HERE TO DELIVER TOYS TO ALL THE KIDS IN THE WORLD, OF COURSE!

SORRY SANTA, BUT MONEY'S TIGHT THESE DAYS, WE CAN'T AFFORD TO LET YOU GIVE OUT ALL THESE FREE PRESENTS AND DEPRIVE OUR STORES OF CHRISTMAS TOY SALES.

WH-?! B-BUT I-..!

BLAM!

..AND THAT'S WHY THERE WON'T BE ANY PRESENTS THIS YEAR!

"If you think that's bad. Wait til you hear about the Easter Bunny.

He was originally going to hide the cat in his mouth,
but there was no room next to the badger.

WHEN YOU'RE ON A DATE AT A RESTAURANT, A GREAT WAY TO IMPRESS THE GIRL IS TO PUT ON A SHOW AS YOU EAT.

CHECK THIS OUT.

A FAVOURITE OF MINE IS TO SWALLOW A FRIED EGG WHOLE.

THOUGH SOMETIMES YOU MIGHT PUT IT IN YOUR MOUTH AT A FUNNY ANGLE, RENDERING THE SWALLOWING PROCESS QUITE DIFFICULT.

IF THIS HAPPENS. SPITTING THE EGG BACK ON TO THE PLATE IS **NOT AN OPTION!**

GIRLS AREN'T INTERESTED IN QUITTERS. YOU GOTTA SHOW YOUR COMMITMENT.

YOU CAN'T GIVE UP UNTIL THAT EGG IS SWALLOWED!

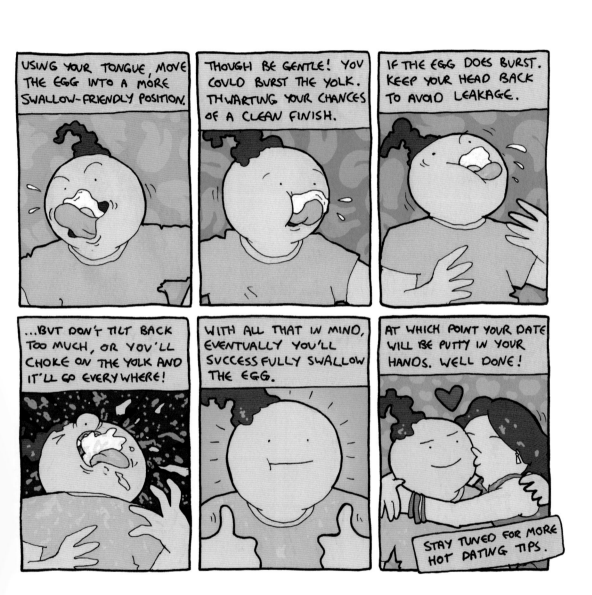

Even if the egg is already in prime swallowing position. You would do well to move the egg around with your tongue anyway. As it is a great opportunity to show your date how great you are with your tongue. For bonus points, throw them a lustful gaze as you shift that mischievous egg.

Other creatures to watch out for: USB cable snakes, invisible hippo

Frosty The 'Froman. He was a jolly happy soul singer.

Prequel to the comic on page 27. No amount of jail-time will jar his love for that shirt

If only he went with a less offensive swear word, like CRAP. Then he'd only have to give up an eyeball (or an eyedot in this case).

He's gonna have to start using his feet! .. FOR THE SCULPTING, I MEANT FOR SCULPTING

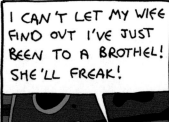

"Haha oh man, I can't believe it worked. She has no idea!"

He may not have the key for it, but I'm sure he could just pry it open if he wanted to.
But he doesn't, because he has a huge fetish for unopened treasure chests.

She should have talked in a smaller font.

To be honest, this comic isn't REALLY just for the ladies. I'm up for whatever

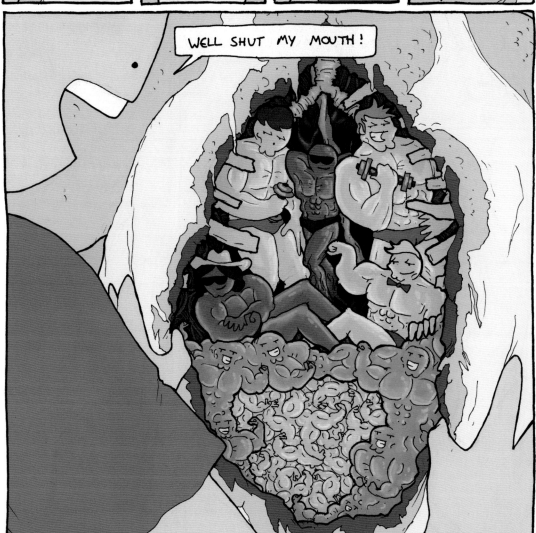

I'm not warping the phrase's meaning at all. Those organ hunks have wonderful personalities.

He was lucky to get that refund. Usually you have to provide a receipt and/or vomit the food back into its original packaging.

He then apologised for breaking the door, because it is also super manly to admit when you've been careless.

The fun part to this is reading the comic out loud as fast as you can, whilst successfully pronouncing every bass correctly.

He is soooo not getting that Shiva materia.

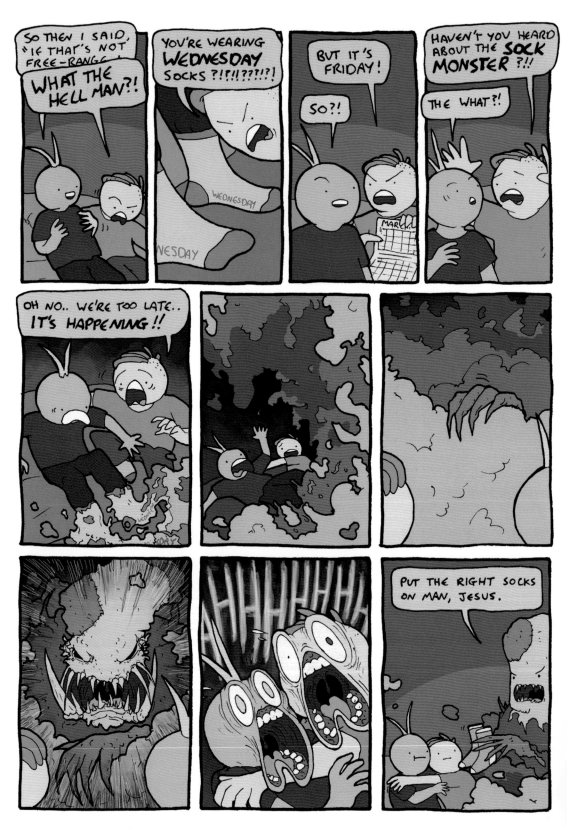

The monster used to have a day-specific sock for a head, but he soon grew tired of having to transfer his brain from sock to sock 7 times a week.

The truth card reads as follows: "Ugh what are you doing? Pick dare you idiot."

Despite only having one foot. Bigfoot still managed to escape as Phil and Murv got distracted by a passing blue tit.

The 'Burnt Art Abandoned in the Park' installation quickly became a town favourite as it brilliantly captured the frustrations of failure. Hearing of its success, Simmer rushed out to claim credit. Only to find out that the hype was just a clever ploy by the local police to identify the person responsible for illegally burning waste. Busted.

"But Dan, this comic makes no sense, surely it should work both ways in that all the while nothing is put in the box, it would constantly generate something." Yes. But surely air counts as something? BOOM!! Next question.

Three records were broken that day: Longest sex, longest post-sex smoking session and longest time spent knocking one out in a traffic cone costume.

WELL HEY THERE! GOT ANY COOL BOOK IDEAS FOR ME?

ABSOLUTELY! SAY HELLO TO...

PUTTERBUTT!!

THE HOLESOME ADVENTURES OF PUTTERBUTT

SURELY **BUTT PUTT** WOULD BE A CATCHIER TITLE?

BUT THAT WOULD BE DECEIVING! THE STORY IS ABOUT A **BUTT** THAT **PUTTS.**

"BUTT PUTT" WOULD IMPLY THAT THE STORY INVOLVES PUTTING BUTTS!

Putt, flop and fart: The lesser-known but far more effective alternative to stop, drop and roll.

Deep.

First prize is a framed photo of the winner receiving the prize.

IF YOU EVER FIND YOURSELF WONDERING WHAT TO DO FOR A DATE. TAKE THEM FISHING.

IT MAY SEEM LIKE A RISKY CHOICE AT FIRST, BUT IT'LL PAY OFF.

AFTER ALL, IT IS A WIDELY KNOWN FACT THAT THE AMOUNT OF FISH YOU CAN CATCH IN A DAY IS A DIRECT INDICATOR OF HOW GOOD YOU ARE IN BED.

THAT SAID, IN THE LIKELY EVENT THAT YOU FAIL TO CATCH A SINGLE FISH, AND THE DAY PROVES HORRENDOUSLY BORING...

EVENTUALLY YOUR DATE MIGHT SUDDENLY BLURT OUT SOMETHING LIKE:

HAHA MAN, WE SHOULD TOTALLY HAVE SEX IN THIS BOAT.

DON'T LET IT THROW YOU. IT'S A TEST!

Alternatively, if you do catch a fish. Cut off some of the fishing line and make your date a fish head necklace. They'll love it. A souvenir of your time together will ensure that they'll never forget you. And hey, maybe 50 years down the line, they'll invite you to their place for a bit of hot sexy strip bingo.

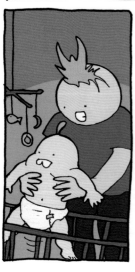

It's not so bad. I think there's a rattle in there too

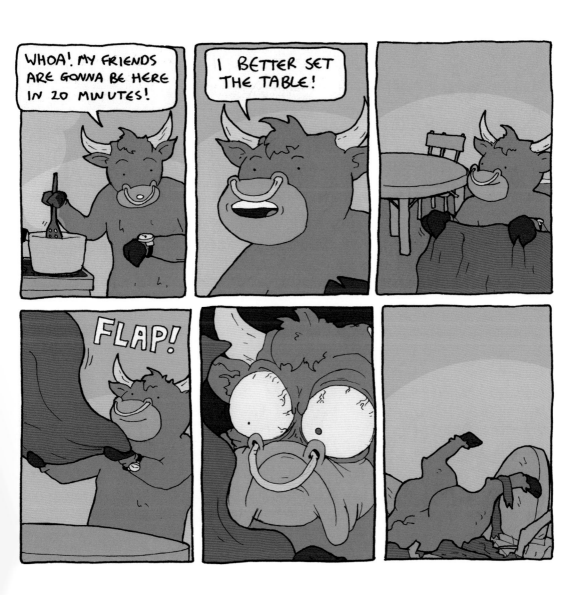

It's not actually the colour red that enrages the bull. It's the constant reminder that they'll never get to wear those fabulous matador costumes.

It also comes with a state-of-the-art alarm clock feature; there's a butt on the other side that farts into your wrist at the set time. It may sound silly, but it is the future. The loudest alarm noises pale in comparison to the effectiveness of dual-cheek vibration

It's not just a t-shirt, it's a warning. Fire isn't the only thing that can issue sick burns.

At least she didn't catch him with that naughty magazine again

It's a shame he didn't bust out his special bass fish sunglasses instead. Cause hey, might as well COVER ALL BASSES!!!! HA HA THERE IT IS AGAIN. SOMEBODY STOP ME.

This is the real reason why I quit my job. None of that "pursuing the dream" rubbish

What's your bra size? DOUBLE I ?? Heh heh heh .. *ahem*

Great shirt choice. The orange really brings out the flames on his burning face.

196

So yeah, if you have head lice, consider waiting it out. You might get a trophy!

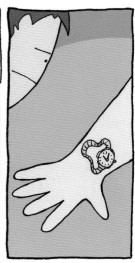

Okay, it was dumb to trust Brunswick with the accompanying text last time. But I believe in second chances. So I've left him in charge of sticking ₹50 notes in every copy of this book as a surprise thank you to the fans.

Why check your phone now? You'll have plenty of time for that in your coffin when I BURY YOU ALIVE.

Sandal sales went through the roof after that water walking publicity stunt.

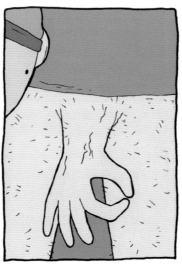

The doctor prescribed him with 50mgs of "Kick Me" stickers,
to be applied to the back on a daily basis.

They really crossed the line with this on

The other guy was sentenced to 5 years in a maximum
security prison to improve his sense of humour.

"...and take that balaclava off! I'm not letting you drive without adequate peripheral vision."

Hey don't worry, this almost never happens in real life.

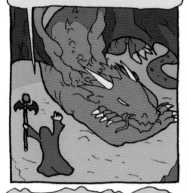

"But but but... I'll feel the spider walking around on the other side of the paper!
Ahh that'll feel so weird on my hand!! OH GOD I CAN'T DO IT."

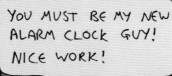

Alarm clock guy was no longer invited to curry night

...and so, Goopy spent the rest of the day lying in the grass, soaking up the sun with a smile on his face and everyone lived happily ever after.

Later that day, a picture of the girl dropping books everywhere was posted online with "FAIL" written in the corner. Book-dropper girl become an overnight sensation

DEATHBULGE FASHION TIPS FOR SUMMER

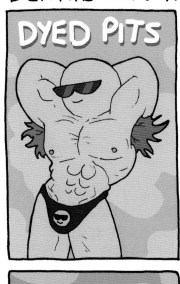

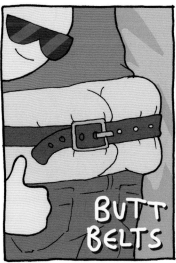

Word on the street is that there are people who are surgically adding extra nostrils to their face so that they can pull off the highly celebrated Triple Booger Saver.

THE ULTIMATE WAY TO EAT ICE CREAM

FIRST THINGS FIRST. GET YOUR HANDS ON A BIG TUB OF ICE CREAM. A BUCKET IF POSSIBLE.

...AND START EATING. NO NEED TO DO ANYTHING FANCY, JUST KEEP EATING.

SOON YOU'LL BE HIT WITH SOME RATHER NASTY BRAIN FREEZE.

BUT DON'T LET THAT STOP YOU. EMBRACE THE PAIN. KEEP GOING. KEEP EATING MORE ICE CREAM!!

EVENTUALLY THE BRAIN FREEZE WILL BECOME SO INTENSE THAT IT'LL COURSE THROUGH YOUR ENTIRE BODY.

...AND YOU WILL BE FROZEN SOLID.

AFTER A MILLENIUM OR TWO, YOU'LL BE WOKEN UP BY SOME FUTURISTIC-LOOKING PEOPLE.

THEY'LL MOST LIKELY CARRY OUT SOME WEIRD TESTS ON YOU FOR A FEW WEEKS.

BUT SOONER OR LATER YOU'LL BE LET OUT. LEAVING YOU FREE TO ENJOY THE MANY PERKS OF LIFE IN THE FUTURE!

...LIKE GOING TO THE BANK AND SEEING THE INSANE AMOUNT OF INTEREST THAT HAS BEEN ADDED TO YOUR ACCOUNT OVER TIME.

£539,485

FOLLOWED BY THE THRILL OF REALISING THAT THE RATE OF INFLATION CANCELS THAT OUT.

BARGAIN BURGERS ONLY £99999!!

YOU COULD ALSO TAKE ADVANTAGE OF THE PHOTOSHOP SURGERY.

..SO YOU CAN LOOK JUST LIKE YOUR FAVOURITE CELEBRITY.

OR YOU COULD CHECK OUT HOW ALL YOUR FRIENDS DIED. THAT'S FUN TOO.

— SLAPPED REALLY HARD
— EATEN BY COW
— DROWNED IN MONEY
— CRUSHED BY COFFIN
— UNDER-EXPOSURE TO SEGA BASS FISHING
— DIDN'T PLEDGE ON THE DEATHBULGE KICKSTARTER
— RELAXED TO DEATH BY LISTENING TO TOO MUCH SMOOTH JAZZ
— FELL OVER WHILST IN A HIGH-GRAVITY SIMULATOR
— DECAPITATED BY OWN NECK
— SWALLOWED CHEWING GUM CHEWED SWALLOWING GUM
— DIDN'T LEVEL UP ENOUGH BEFORE FIGHTING THAT BOSS

Deathbulge's Photo Manipulation Program is now open for business. So if you'd like your significant other to have my face in all your wedding photos. That can be arranged.

Confessing to your parents that you're straight is one of the hardest things you'll ever have to do.

He soon calmed down after hearing the soothing tones of someone saying that a duck's quack always echoes.

It's a shame he never got round to installing those flaming hoops inside.

He should probably switch to a short-sleeved shirt to avoid further melting.

You got a thesaurus back there too? It'd be a bit boring to just keep calling you a slag over and over. Would be nice to cycle through some synonyms. Keep it fresh, y'know?

Believe it or not, this DOES actually happen in real life. I make sure of it. Also, word on the street is that the gems have assumed the form of Deathbulge merchandise.

"Man, this is great. Why doesn't EVERYONE do this?"

"I can't believe they saw my hair before it was fully flowered. How embarrassing." :(

Just like with the 100th comic, red text indicates lines of dialogue that were suggested by readers.

AS THE SEA TURNED LAVENDER WITH RAGE...

... AND THE CLIFFS BEGAN TO CRUMBLE.

HE SOON REALIZED THE DREADFUL MISTAKE HE HAD MADE WITH THE PARSLEY.

I TRUSTED YOU..

EHH, I DON'T LIKE THIS PLOT TWIST. IT'S NOT DRAMATIC ENOUGH.

GOOD SHOW THOUGH.

HELP!! HELP!!!!

SOMEONE'S IN TROUBLE!

RENT AN ISOPOD

YEAH NO SHIT, MAYBE YOU SHOULD GO HELP THEM.

YOU ALRIGHT?

NO!!

MY LAB HAS BEEN OVER-RUN WITH GIANT RATS!

YOU GOTTA HELP ME GET RID OF THEM!

HANG ON MATE. WHAT'S IN IT FOR US?

I WILL MAKE SURE YOU ARE HANDSOMELY REWARDED.

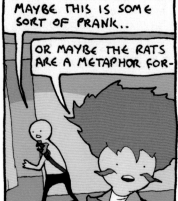

ALL IT TAKES IS SOME SWEET-ASS MOVES AND **TWO GOOD FISTS!**

DOOF!

THUD!

AW JEEZ,

YEAH WE'RE SCREWED.

IT'S A SHAME WE NEVER ACTUALLY GOT ROUND TO MAKING ANY MUSIC.

SHUNK!

WHAT.

SLICE!

WHO **IS** THAT?!

LOOKS LIKE SOME SORT OF LLAMA!

LLAMA... WHY DOES THAT...?

OH NO..

OH NO!!

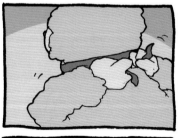
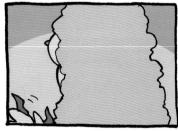

HELLO SON!

URRRGGH!!!

SORRY SIMMER. WE JUST DIDN'T WANNA INTERFERE WITH YOUR FATHER AND SON BONDING SESSION.

YOU CAN COME OUT NOW PROFESSOR.

Y- YOU GOT THEM ?!

WELL, MY DAD DID MOST OF THE WORK.

OH.. SO WHO AM I GIVING THE REWARD TO ?

YOU GUYS CAN HAVE IT.

ARE YOU SURE ?!

KNOWING MY SON IS ALRIGHT IS REWARD ENOUGH FOR ME.

WELL, ALRIGHT THEN! THANKS FOR YOUR HELP AT ANY RATE. HERE IS YOUR REWARD !!

TOUGH BREAK BRO.

I..I DON'T UNDERSTAND.. ..HOW COULD SHE..?

COME ON, LET'S SET-UP OUR NEW TOTEM POLE! THAT'LL TAKE YOUR MIND OFF THINGS!

I PAINTED IT... ALL BY MYSELF..

10 MINUTES LATER...

WOW!!

SAYS HERE THAT EACH TOTEM ON THE POLE IS A SYMBOLIC REPRESENTATION OF ONE FAMILY!

KNOW YOUR TOTEM

Y'KNOW, I NEVER KNEW THAT!

ME NEITHER!

KNOW YOUR TOTE

BOVRIL, DID YOU KNOW THAT??

I NEVER KNEW LOVE FELT LIKE BEING STABBED REPEATEDLY IN THE BACK.

COME ON MAN, DON'T BE LIKE THAT. THERE'S PLENTY MORE FISH IN THE SEA!

YOU'RE.. YOU'RE RIGHT!

I GOTTA GET MYSELF OUT THERE!

233

Bovril went on to achieve great things on Boomboomslap Island. But his adventure isn't over yet. I'll bring B.B.A. back from hiatus someday, you have my word!

Guest comic for Mercworks. Go check out his comics at mercworks.ne—

This comic was created whilst drunk. So if it's your favourite comic in the book then you should send me some wine. Actually, even if it isn't your favourite, send wine.

FIND THE STUFF

People
Alien
Cool dude
Four-armed Man
Ladies kissing
4 x People throwing up
Pirate
Robot
Someone urinating where they shouldn't be.
Stealth Snowman
The Man with a Nose

Animals
3 x Butterflies
Cat
Dog
Fish
Grizzly the Bear
Snake

Objects
Bowling ball
10 x Brown bottles
Burger
Camera
Chainsaw
Mystery box
Party hat
Rubber duck
Skeleton pyjamas
Tennis ball

ABOUT THE AUTHOR

Hello there. I'm Dan Martin! I live in Morden, UK and I'd like to think I'm a fun person to be around.

Alongside my love for drawing, I also enjoy video games, especially platformers and RPGs. In fact one of my ultimate goals in life is to make a Deathbulge-themed RPG game someday; preferably a good one.

I picked the name Deathbulge because the comic started out as a story about a death metal band and when I was brainstorming band names, Deathbulge was the only one that made me giggle.

SPECIAL SKILL: I'm able to identify the flags of all the countries in the world. You should quiz me on that if you ever meet me in person, I will love you for it.

BIRD COMIC CLUE:
Look at the shape of the bird in the last panel, then at the blue sign in the background.